# Elizabethan England

Kathy Elgin

Copyright © 2009 Bailey Publishing Associates Ltd

Produced for Chelsea House by Bailey Publishing Associates Ltd, 11a Woodlands, Hove BN3 6TJ, England

Project Manager: Patience Coster
Text Designer: Jane Hawkins
Picture Research: Shelley Noronha
Artist: Deirdre Clancy Steer

**Library of Congress Cataloging-in-Publication Data**
Elgin, Kathy.
  Elizabethan England / Kathy Elgin.
    p. cm. — (Costume source books)
  Includes bibliographical references and index.
  ISBN 978-1-60413-379-0
  1. Clothing and dress—England—History—16th century—Juvenile literature. 2. England—Social life and customs—16th century—Juvenile literature. I. Title. II. Series.
  GT734.E44 2009
  391.00942'09031—dc22
                        2008047258

Printed and bound in Hong Kong

10 9 8 7 6 5 4 3 2 1

The publishers would like to thank the following for permission to reproduce their pictures: Bailey Publishing Associates Ltd: *contents*, 37, 41; with grateful thanks to Mr J. Berkeley, The Berkeley Will Trust: 24 and 52 *detail*; Bridgeman Art Library: 12 (Hardwick Hall, Derbyshire, UK, National Trust Photographic Library/P. A. Burton), *title page* and 15 (Yale Center for British Art, Paul Mellon Collection, USA), 18 (© Walker Art Gallery, National Museums Liverpool), 34 (Private Collection), 34 *detail*, and 40 (Hatfield House, Hertfordshire, UK), 42 (Grimsthorpe Castle, Lincolnshire, UK), 44 (© Yale Center for British Art, Paul Mellon Fund, USA), 48 (Private Collection, Photo © Christie's Images), 5 *detail*, 48 *detail*, and 49 (Longleat House, Wiltshire, UK), 50 (Private Collection, Photo © Rafael Valls Gallery, London, UK), 59 (© Ashmolean Museum, University of Oxford, UK); Martyn F. Chillmaid: 26, 35, 37, 39, 43; Corbis: 6 (© The Gallery Collection); Mary Evans Picture Library: 8, 14; Kobal Collection: 32 (Columbia); *Much Ado About Nothing* (2004)/John Tramper/Shakespeare's Globe: 53; NTPL: 33 Elizabeth Hardwick Countess of Shrewsbury (Bess of Hardwick), attr. to Rowland Lockey, Hardwick Hall, The Devonshire Collection, acquired through the National Land Fund and transferred to The National Trust in 1959, ©NTPL/John Bethell); Rex Features: 9 (Miramax/Everett),10, 11, 30, 52; Topfoto: 5, 18 *detail*, and 19 (KPA/HIP/Topfoto), (ArenaPal/Topfoto), 13 (HIP), 20 (KPA), 22, 21 (ArenaPal/Topfoto), 23 (ArenaPal/Topfoto), 27 (ArenaPal/Topfoto), 28 (ArenaPal/Topfoto), 36 (ArenaPal/Topfoto), 38 (Thos F. Holte & Mig Holte Collection/Arp/Topfoto), 46 (J. Abecasis Collection/ Topfoto), 47 (Thos F. Holte & Mig Holte Collection, © Shakespeare Birthplace Trust/ArenaPal/Topfoto), 54 (Art Media/HIP/Topfoto), 55 (PA/Topfoto), 56 (Print Collector/HIP/Topfoto); Victoria and Albert Museum: *title page detail*, *imprint* and *contents page detail*, 6 *detail*, 10 *detail*, 26 *detail*, 42 *detail*, 67, 16, 31, 57, 58 (V&A Images).

# Contents

# Introduction

The Elizabethan period was one of the most glamorous in English history. Not only was the country enjoying a period of economic expansion and political dominance, but Queen Elizabeth I herself was a style icon admired and imitated all over Europe.

This book will focus on the period approximately between 1550 and 1603, which takes us from the end of the Tudor period, when Elizabeth was a young princess, to her death in 1603. These are not random dates. Although, of course, fashions did not change overnight with the accession of the young queen in 1558, "Elizabethan" fashion is clearly very different from the solid, somewhat top-heavy style of Elizabeth's father, King Henry VIII, and even that of her half sister, Queen Mary. And the fashions of King James I and the Stuarts, who followed the Elizabethan period, were different again. Although the terms Tudor and Elizabethan are sometimes used interchangeably, it's important to get these distinctions right in any production or re-enactment where it really matters. Also, when embarking on costuming, it's important to establish at the outset the class and location of the character you are dressing before any decision about style, fabric, or pattern is made.

We know a lot about Elizabethan clothing, thanks to the many portraits that were painted and the written documents that list items in minute detail. These are invaluable to the researcher. We can also glean much from the theater. In Shakespeare's plays especially, references to fabrics, styles of clothing, jokes about extreme fashion, and so on, occur in unexpected places—even in high tragedy. This suggests that his audience, both high- and low-born, would be immediately familiar with the references. Unfortunately, many of these fascinating references are often cut from productions today because they have become obscure.

## FRILLS AND FANCIES

*" And now, my honey love,*
*We will return unto thy father's house,*
*And revel it as bravely as the best,*
*With silken coats and caps, and golden rings,*
*With ruffs and cuffs and farthingales and things,*
*With scarfs and fans, and double change*
*    of bravery,*
*With amber bracelets, beads, and all this*
*    knavery. "*

William Shakespeare, *The Taming of the Shrew*, c.1596

# CHAPTER 1

# The Elizabethan World

## THE WOOL TRADE

England had long been a leader in the wool trade, and by Elizabeth's time wool cloth represented 90 percent of the country's exports. The mainstay of the country's economy, the trade had to be carefully protected. However, most of the cloth went to the Netherlands, which at that time was a province of Spain. Since political relations between England and Spain were precarious at best, the stability of the wool trade was of constant concern throughout the Elizabethan period. This explains some of the strange laws and statutes compelling people to wear wool clothes, and especially caps, in order to boost trade.

## THE CHARACTER OF ENGLAND

Outside London, Elizabethan England was still basically an agricultural society. There were only about three million people—fewer, in fact, than 200 years before, when the Black Death had claimed the lives of about 40 percent of the population. The largest city outside London was Norwich, with 15,000 people. Most of the English population lived in the countryside or, increasingly, in one of the 800 or so market towns scattered around the central and southern part of the country. By today's standards, these towns were small. A place like Stratford-upon-Avon, Shakespeare's birthplace, had perhaps a dozen streets and 200 families—probably 1,000 people in all. Northern England was still a wild region, poorly served by trade and inaccessible for travel. London, however, was a city booming with commerce. Trade of all kinds, especially in cloth and clothing, was flourishing.

*Below:* Portraits of Queen Elizabeth presented her not just as beautiful and wealthy but as an almost mythical figure, surrounded by symbols of her country's power and authority. In the background of this painting are scenes showing England defeating the Spanish Armada.

Society was divided between aristocracy and commoners but increasingly also between old "country" and new "town." The rise of the middle classes—merchants, bankers, builders, and traders of many kinds—went on relentlessly. All these changes had an effect on clothing. As more people could afford better fabrics, they were imported in greater quantities than ever before. The home production of some items was also being established, thanks to foreign craftsmen who had settled in English towns, bringing their skills with them.

## CHANGING STYLES

Tudor clothing developed from the two main medieval garments, the houppelande and the cotehardie. A version of the loose houppelande, now pleated and belted at the waist, became the main male garment, while the women's close-fitting cotehardie had developed into the kirtle, a one-piece dress that fit closely over bodice and hips, then fell into full, floor-length skirts. A gown of similar design could be worn over this.

Most Europeans wore more or less the same kind of clothing, made from the same fabrics, as they had throughout the medieval and early Renaissance periods. Fabrics ranged from the staple wool and linen, worn by all classes, to luxury fabrics such as silk, velvet, and brocades, imported from the East or Italy and worn by the wealthy. The title of medieval style leader had passed between the various princely courts—mainly those of Burgundy in France and wealthy Italian dynasties such as the Medici in Florence. By the first half of the sixteenth century, German fashions were all the rage, with an emphasis on bright, even garish, colors.

During Henry VIII's time, the silhouette was generally a rather squashed, flattened one, especially in men's wear, where the shoulders were greatly exaggerated. Gowns were voluminous, with huge sleeves;

*Above:* Members of Sir Thomas More's family are wearing various styles of Tudor fashion, depending on their ages. The younger women, at the front, are dressed in the height of fashion.

## THE ROYAL WARDROBE

The Great Wardrobe was the court office responsible for the monarch's clothing and household effects. It commissioned items from specialist craftspeople, including tailors, hatmakers, furriers, embroiderers, jewelers, and those who made garments for hunting, riding, and playing sports. It was a huge undertaking whose offices, by Elizabeth's time, occupied an entire street. The Great Wardrobe's careful accounts of who made what and when, the fabrics used, and how much each item cost have been invaluable to costume historians.

During the Elizabethan era, many writers published pamphlets commenting on their life and times. One of these was Philip Stubbes (c.1555–c.1610), a strict Puritan who had very firm views on any social practices he regarded as immoral. His work *The Anatomie of Abuses* (1583) includes attacks on the extremes of Elizabethan fashion— extravagant farthingales, over-decorated shirts, and enormous ruffs—aimed particularly at the aspiring middle classes. Two other important sources of information are John Stow's *Survey of London* (1598) and William Harrison's *The Description of England* (1587).

hats and shoes were wide and flat. Heavy, large-patterned fabrics, often woven with metallic thread, and fur trimmings and linings remained popular.

## SPANISH STYLE

When Henry VIII married Katherine of Aragon in 1509, the Spanish princess brought with her a new style, which was quickly adopted by English women. At court, at least, the flowing kirtle was replaced by a cone-shaped skirt, held out from the body by hooped undergarments, and a stiffened bodice. Crucially, the one-piece gown was now separated into several distinct items—bodice, skirt, sleeves—and would remain so for at least a century.

With the marriage of Katherine's daughter, Queen Mary, to Philip II of Spain in 1554, the reign of Spanish fashion was confirmed. Now that Henry himself was gone, the influence spread quickly to men's fashion as well as women's. This was already the case in much of Europe, where courtiers had been eager to imitate the style of the Spanish Holy Roman emperors. Suddenly, the youth of England were wearing short,

*Right:* This illustration shows a Spanish noble couple from about 1550. The lady's skirt is fastened down the front, instead of revealing the kirtle, and her sleeves are very ornate, while the man's outfit is quite restrained.

tight doublets that revealed equally brief breeches and hose. And almost everyone wore black, favored by the famously austere Philip.

## THE ELIZABETHANS

The new queen's accession ushered in a whole new epoch of style and elegance. Her long reign was a period of relative prosperity that gave people the opportunity to amass fortunes and to concentrate on clothes, fashion, and enjoying themselves. The idea of displaying one's wealth through clothing and possessions reached a new prominence.

Fashion began at court, then rippled outward through the aristocracy and minor nobility to the socially aspiring middle classes. Working folk, on the whole, had neither time nor money for fashion. The speed at which fashions changed at court was astonishing. Although the basic shapes remained the same, fine-tuning the details of sleeve and neckline were key in the race to keep abreast of fashion. However, in the absence of fashion magazines and news broadcasts, it could take months, even years, for a new style to find its way to the far-flung areas, especially the north. Country people and less well-off townsfolk wore their Tudor styles well into the new period.

The costumes for the movie *Shakespeare in Love* were well researched. Gwyneth Paltrow's low-necked gold brocade gown is typical of those fashionable in the 1590s.

## LIFE IN THE SPOTLIGHT

To the Elizabethans, life was a continual performance in which clothes played the major part. This was true for men even more than women. No one could succeed at court or in business without the right outfit, and wearing last month's fashion was frowned on. It wasn't unknown for courtiers to bankrupt their families through extravagant expenditures on clothing.

## A NOTE ON MAKING CLOTHES

Better tailoring and more sophisticated cutting tools meant that clothes could be cut in clever ways, with curved seams and fitted bodices. Consequently, these clothes are a little harder to reproduce than the earlier styles. However, many online agencies offer patterns and advice on fabrics.

## THE ELIZABETHAN STAGE

Elizabethan actors performed in slightly more elaborate versions of ordinary clothes, with the addition of a few props to indicate character or status. Monarchs wore crowns, for example, and a shepherd might carry a crook, while a man wearing a long gown was probably a doctor. For "traditional" re-creations, the same rules can be followed today. However, an Elizabethan stage gown was made of expensive fabric and often cost more than the child actor wearing it was paid in a year.

## WARDROBE WORRIES

Clearly the queen had to be the best-dressed person at court, and she changed her costume several times a day. This involved some effort on the part of her wardrobe-keepers. The queen's wardrobe accounts for 1600 listed the following new garments:
99 robes, 102 French gowns, 67 round gowns, 100 loose gowns, 126 kirtles [underskirts], 136 foreparts [stomachers], 125 petticoats, 96 cloaks, 43 safeguards [protective overskirts], 85 doublets, 18 lap mantles [shawls], 27 fans, and nine pantofles [slippers or overshoes]. Each item had to be kept clean and in top condition in case the queen decided to wear it. Fortunately, most of today's fabrics are easy to wash, but it pays to check!

# Women's Wear at Court

## THE TUDOR SILHOUETTE

The basic women's costume consists of a linen smock, then the kirtle, a one-piece dress worn over the smock, and over that a gown.

The defining elements are the square neckline, deep bell sleeves, and the angular gable headdress. A typical gown has sleeves that fit close at the top of the arm and hang wide at the wrist, revealing the closer-fitting sleeve of the kirtle. The neckline is square, cut very wide to the shoulder and edged with a band of embroidery or gems. The bodice is fitted to the waist and the skirt bell-shaped, usually open at the front to reveal an undergarment of contrasting pattern. A girdle, made of silken rope or padded silk, was hung low around the waist. It was tied in a knot at the front and had various items attached to it. Trains, popular throughout the medieval period, gradually shortened and were looped up at the back until, by about 1540, they had disappeared completely.

*Below:* In *Elizabeth R,* Glenda Jackson played the queen at all stages of her life, from teenage princess, seen here in her late-Tudor fashions, to old age.

*Above:* In this scene from *The Other Boleyn Girl*, both Scarlett Johansson (left), as Mary, and Natalie Portman, as Anne, are wearing French hoods.

An alternative to the gable headdress was the French hood, a favorite of Mary, Queen of Scots, and of Anne Boleyn, Henry VIII's second wife, both of whom had spent time at the French court. Both headdresses were made of stiffened buckram wired into shape and covered with fabric, which was then edged with strips of pearls or other jewels, called billiments. A black veil, attached to the back, hung down to the shoulders in both cases, but whereas the gable sat on the forehead, hiding the hair completely, the French hood sat farther back on the crown of the head and revealed the hair, parted in the center. Both could be covered with fabric to match the gown, although a discreet black velvet was very popular for the French hood.

## THE ELIZABETHANS

The keynote for Elizabethan women's wear is stiffness. Ironically, many of the fabrics themselves were light and soft—silk, satin, gauzes of various kinds—but the boning and padding that gave the requisite artificiality, exaggerating the tiny waist and emphasizing hips and upper body, restricted the wearer's movement considerably. These were not clothes to

relax in, and this should be remembered when re-creating them: movies that show ladies running around carelessly in full court dress should be taken with a grain of salt.

## FARTHINGALES

The farthingale dictated the basic Elizabethan shape. The earliest was the Spanish version, which gave the bell shape of Tudor and early Elizabethan skirts. It was a series of concentric hoops sewn into an underskirt, increasing in size from waist to floor. Originally, these would have been made of wire, rope, or, a little later, whalebone. The first two, at least, could be used today, but hoopskirt boning is now available from suppliers. Cotton, or drill, is the best material to use: cheaper or lightweight acetates won't survive the wear and tear.

After about 1590, the French farthingale became popular. This was a wheel-shaped structure whose metal spokes held the skirt straight out from the hips so that it fell sharply to the floor. Queen Elizabeth liked this fashion, but it was much mocked by writers of the time, who made jokes about women with skirts too wide to pass through doorways.

## BODICE AND SKIRT

Bodices were close-fitting and boned. From about 1570, a decorative panel, or "stomacher," was worn at the front, either sewn or laced in. During pregnancy—a significant part of their lives—women left off the stomacher but still laced the gown, as one sees from many portraits. The breasts were completely flattened but often visible above the neckline. Today's strapless push-up bras are a godsend in this respect, unless you're going for scrupulous accuracy. Skirts were often open from the waist to reveal the kirtle skirt in contrasting fabric. For simpler re-creations, a sewn-in panel of contrasting fabric will do.

## NECKWEAR

Ruffs came in all shapes and sizes, from a single teardrop twist to multilayered cartwheels that stuck out about 12 inches (30 centimeters) from the neck. They were made of fine, gauzy linen and had to be starched to make them stand up properly, although they were supported by a wire "supportasse" underneath. Web sites give many variations of

## THE ETIQUETTE OF COLOR

Traditionally, purple and bright red had been reserved for royalty and the nobility, mostly because the dyes required were difficult to obtain and prohibitively expensive. Elizabethan sumptuary laws attempted to regulate who was allowed to wear what, but there were less obvious "rules." Woe betide any courtier who wore black and white or black and silver. These were the queen's colors, permitted only to herself and special favorites such as the Earl of Leicester. In her later years, pastel shades of peach and lemon were the fashion, irrespective of whether or not such colors suited the virile young men wearing them.

*Below:* French fashions of the period show even more variations on bodice, sleeves, and neckline. Courtiers and ambassadors carried fashion news quickly from one court to another.

## AN AUDIENCE WITH THE QUEEN

"She was strangely attired in a dress of silver cloth, white and crimson, or silver 'gauze', as they call it. This dress had slashed sleeves lined with red taffeta, and was girt about with other little sleeves that hung down to the ground. . . . The collar of the robe was very high, and the lining of the inner part all adorned with little pendants of rubies and pearls, very many but quite small. She also had a chain of rubies and pearls about her neck. On her head she wore a garland of the same material and beneath it a great reddish-coloured wig, with a great number of spangles of gold and silver, and hanging down over her forehead some pearls."

Sieur de Maisse, a French envoy to the English court in 1597–8, recorded his first sight of Queen Elizabeth

*Above:* Ruffs could be worn in many styles, depending on age and status.

possible style for ruffs. Wide organza ribbon is a good choice since it needs no hemming, but a strip of linen cut along the selvage is good too and can also be starched.

Once ruffs had become outrageously wide, in about 1580, women began to wear them differently. Instead of enclosing the neck, the ends were pinned to the shoulders of the wide neckline so that the ruff stood up like a fan. Generally, these were worn by unmarried women: wives usually limited themselves to a neat, closed ruff.

### FASTENINGS

Laces, ties, buttons, and brooches all served a useful purpose, but making these into decorative features became an art in itself. Seams were often covered up with a silver lace: at the shoulder, where sleeve met bodice, a raised and decorative stuffed band covered the join. Rows of tiny buttons might follow the front seam of a bodice, even if none of them actually undid. These are easy ways of adding interest to a garment today, even if the actual fastening has been faked with Velcro or a zipper.

### UNDERWEAR

A fine linen shift, sometimes left visible at the neck, was the only undergarment. Drawers would not be worn for another century or so. A kind of boned corset maintained the flattened shape, known as "a pair

Black work was embroidery in which geometric shapes were worked in black thread on a white background, usually linen. It was often called "poor man's lace" because from a distance it resembled the more expensive bobbin lace, produced in the Netherlands, which often decorated collars and cuffs. An even cheaper and quicker alternative is to draw the design on with a fine black felt-tip or washable paint.

*Left:* The bodice of this gorgeous black-work dress plunges deep into the skirt, which is supported by a French farthingale. This is thought to be a portrait of Mary Clopton of Kentwell Hall, Suffolk.

of bodies" because it had a front and a back. This was stiffened with whalebone and laced up the front. Today, the effect is better achieved by stiffening the bodice itself, unless one really wants to wear a corset.

## THE LATER YEARS

After 1580, styles became even more exaggerated. Along with the French farthingale went huge sleeves and even tinier waists. The point of the bodice and stomacher now extended below the natural waist, descending into a deep V at hip level. Ruffs were also getting out of hand, with the most extreme extending almost a foot out from the neck. Fashion and comfort had long ago parted company!

*Above:* This fabric is "corded"—silk cord overstitched with thread—and embroidered with tiny glass beads to give it a heavy, stiff texture.

## STARCHING

Starching was unknown in England until about 1564, when a Dutch woman named Dinghen van den Plass arrived in London with a recipe for a new substance that would stiffen the fine linen used for ruffs. Her starch was made of wheat or corn flour mixed with water. She charged an enormous sum of money to teach her secrets to English servants and washerwomen, who were soon setting up in business along the banks of the Thames River, washing and starching the fashionable ruffs of gentlefolk. Once starched, the ruff had to be set on sticks to dry into the correct shape.

## FABRICS

The heavy patterned fabrics beloved of the Tudors can be reproduced using furnishing fabrics, which often come in the requisite large patterns. Small-patterned or sprigged fabrics are not authentic. Damask curtain material is ideal. When velvet or satin were used, the fabric itself was usually of a plain, solid color—the effect came from contrasting it with a patterned undergarment or trimming it with braid or lace. Plain fabrics were also the best background for embroidery or sewn-on jewels.

Satin, brocade, and velvet were originally made of silk, but all have their modern, synthetic variants. Although they lack the richness of the original, these are much cheaper and will generally serve their purpose unless you're into serious re-enactment. Cotton velvet, however, gives a better effect than rayon velvet, which can look shiny and is slippery to sew. Elizabethan silk was fine and smooth, so avoid raw silk or anything with a visible texture. Asian fabric suppliers are a good source of silks as well as lightweight gauzes, which will substitute for cloth of gold.

## PORTRAITS

Portraits are an obvious source of information for costumers. Beware, however, when taking references from portraits. Painters often flattered their sitters, exaggerating certain features and playing down others, which gives a false impression of some fashions. Also, family portraits were often painted over retrospectively. Figures were added, faces altered, and costume changed to appear more contemporary. In one case, a husband had his new bride's face superimposed on the body of his dead wife, although the clothes remained those of an earlier period. All of this makes accurate dating difficult.

Hair pulled back from forehead and teased into curls; perhaps worn over pads of horsehair

Coronet of gold or silver wire or lace

Drop earring, made of a single pearl

"Open" or standing ruff, made of gauze, attached to the neckline of the bodice

Line of decoration to conceal joining of sleeve to bodice; broad shoulders make the waist appear narrower

Stiffly boned bodice keeps the figure upright

Detachable sleeves, slightly padded or quilted and gathered at the wrist

Point of bodice projecting into the skirt also makes the waist appear narrower

Lace cuff

Skirt of the gown, supported by a Spanish farthingale to give a bell shape

French gown, made of silk or velvet in a plain color

Kirtle, or forepart, in contrasting patterned fabric

Full-length skirt almost conceals the shoes

17

# CHAPTER 3

# Men's Wear at Court

## THE SOLID TUDORS . . .

In men's wear, Henry VIII set the pattern. The general impression is of solid bulk, with the shoulders greatly exaggerated by huge sleeves. It's a style that shouts masculinity, power, and aggression.

## SHOES FOR THE ROYAL FEET

Henry VIII's shoe account for 1525 included ten pairs of English leather boots; ten pairs of Spanish leather buskins (short boots); a pair of velvet buskins; 38 pairs of velvet shoes in purple, black, and crimson; three pairs of slippers in black velvet; three pairs of "arming shoes," for jousting; six pairs of English leather shoes; and another six pairs of shoes in Spanish leather. The sum of four shillings was spent on "leather shoes for football [soccer]," hand-stitched by the royal shoemaker, Cornelius Johnson.

Over the usual linen shirt went a high-necked doublet and then a relatively new overgarment called a jerkin, open in a deep, rounded V down the front to reveal the doublet. It was belted, and the full skirts, which ended just above the knee, parted to reveal the codpiece. A vast knee-length robe was worn over all, with hugely exaggerated, puffed shoulders ending at the elbow. The robe was usually made of velvet, satin, or brocade and was fur lined or trimmed. The plain hose were gartered just below the knee, and shoes were flat and wide.

## . . . AND THE ELEGANT ELIZABETHANS

Once the heaviness of the Tudors had been swept away, men's fashion changed quickly. Queen Elizabeth gathered around her youthful, glamorous, dynamic people, especially young men. In clothing, masculine aggression turned to athletic elegance. Men wanted to show off a narrow

*Left:* The classic portrait of Henry VIII in all his glory.

*Below:* Queen Elizabeth was always surrounded by an entourage of fashionable young men.

## STYLE TIP

Codpieces may attract a deal of humor, but those enormous, stuffed, and decorated ones were seriously out of fashion by the end of Henry's reign. No Elizabethan courtier would have been caught dead wearing one. In Shakespeare's *Two Gentlemen of Verona*, Lucetta, helping her mistress disguise herself as a boy, teases: "What fashion, madam, shall I make your breeches? . . . You must needs have them with a cod-piece. . . . A round hose, madam, now's not worth a pin, unless you have a cod-piece to stick pins on."

## INTERNATIONAL FASHION

*"How oddly he is suited! I think he bought his doublet in Italy, his round hose in France, his bonnet in Germany, and his behaviour every where."*

William Shakespeare, *The Merchant of Venice*, c.1597

*"A Dutchman today, a Frenchman tomorrow, or in the shape of two countries at once, as a German from the waist downward, all slops, and a Spaniard from the hips upward, no doublet."*

William Shakespeare, *Much Ado About Nothing*, c.1598

*Right:* Venetian dandy Bassanio, in the 2004 movie of Shakespeare's *Merchant of Venice*, is wearing paneled trunk hose and, somewhat unusually, suede boots.

waist, broad chest, and long legs, which made them look fit yet graceful. The short doublet and hose were now standard wear for younger men, along with fine linen shirts and linen undergarments and perhaps a cloak. Planning to pass himself off as a lord in *A Mad World, My Masters*, a comedy written by Thomas Middleton and first performed in 1605, the character Follywit remarks: "A French ruff, a thin beard, and a strong perfume will do it."

### HOSE

The term "hose" is confusing. Strictly speaking, it means stockings and was so understood up to Tudor times. Each stocking was attached by ties or laces to the doublet, and the function of the codpiece was to cover up the gap at the join. However, by the Elizabethan period, hose is often

*Right:* The boots and socks in this production of *Rosencrantz and Guildenstern Are Dead* show how a quirky design touch can add modern relevance to a costume.

used to mean stockings and breeches. Sometimes these are referred to as upper hose (breeches) and nether hose (stockings). In women's wear, however, hose always means stockings. In any case, thick colored tights are today's solution.

When it comes to breeches, there are several options. Trunk or round hose were the bulbous shorts that puffed out over the hips and were gathered into a band at the thigh. By the end of the century, this garment was so short it was barely visible under the doublet. Obviously, full-length hose (tights) are worn with this style. But it's not necessary to reveal all. French hose were a slightly longer and semifitted version, also paned and decorated, worn by nobility and the upper classes. Canions—close-fitting knee-length breeches—could be worn alone or under trunk or French hose. A second pair of tights, cut off at the knee and hemmed, would give the same effect for a young courtier or man-about-town character. Colors were restrained. Brown, russet, gray, and green were popular and, later in the reign, lighter tones of pink, including peach.

Older men, now as then, might be happier in Venetians, which were semifitted and reached beneath the knee. Slops or galligaskins were the same length as Venetians but loose and very full, ending in wide, decorative bands of material called "guardes". The baggier versions, however, lack elegance and are more suitable for country squires or townsfolk.

## LINEN

All classes aspired to shirts and underwear made of linen because it wore well and washed to a comfortable softness. Because it didn't take dye well, linen was invariably left "natural," but if left out in the sun after washing, it bleached naturally to white. Linen is easily available and much in fashion today, but it's quite expensive. Fine cotton, unknown to the Elizabethans, is a good alternative, but it doesn't hang in the same way. Fine, handkerchief-weight linen is best if you can afford it.

Elizabethan shirts were big and baggy—the more voluminous the shirt, the finer the quality. "My shirts I'll have of taffeta-sarsnet, soft and light as cobwebs," declares vain Sir Epicure Mammon in Ben Jonson's satirical play *The Alchemist* (sarsnet, or sarcenet, is a soft silk cloth). The shirts were embroidered, frequently with white-on-white work (white stitching

*Right:* Joseph Fiennes as Robert Dudley, Earl of Leicester in the film *Elizabeth* wears a linen shirt decorated with panels of drawn-thread work.

## A ROW ABOUT SHIRTS

In *Henry IV, Part 1*, Mistress Quickly has an argument with Falstaff about some shirts she's given him as a present. "I bought you a dozen of shirts," she says, to which Falstaff replies: "Dowlas, filthy dowlas. I have given them away to bakers' wives; they have made bolsters of them." Mistress Quickly is outraged: "Now, as I am true woman, holland of eight shillings an ell [meter]!" She's quite right. There's a big difference between the expensive, fine Dutch linen ("holland") Mistress Quickly is claiming and the coarser "dowlas," which was usually used for aprons, sheeting, or, as Falstaff says, bolsters. The quality of linen was a hot topic in Elizabethan times.

on white fabric), and trimmed with lace. Smocking—embroidery over tiny pleats of gathered fabric—was also popular at the neck and cuffs. Women's blouses, in the largest size, will do well today, although a simple shirt is not hard to make.

## PADDING

In order to achieve an exaggerated silhouette, garments were padded with a variety of substances generally known as bombast. This could be anything from horsehair, flocks, and sheep's wool to old rags. Remember, though, that padding causes discomfort. The stuffing down the front of a peascod doublet, popular in the 1570s and 1580s, made it impossible to bend over, and it's hard to sit comfortably in padded trunk hose. These clothes are also very heavy and hot to wear, so if you must pad, compromise with a lightweight stuffing.

## SLASHING

Slashing meant cutting slits in the top clothing and pulling through bunches of fabric from an underlayer in a contrasting color. The fashion originated in Germany and arrived in England during Henry's reign but continued to go in and out of fashion, for both sexes, well into the Elizabethan period. Sometimes the cuts extended into long slashes, which were called panes. Hose cut in this way was very fashionable. It's easy but time-consuming to reproduce; a similar effect can be achieved with a bold striped fabric.

## THE OVERALL EFFECT

Formality was the watchword of the Elizabethans. Doublets were rarely unbuttoned, and paintings show that men of most classes kept their hats on indoors, even in their own houses. In Shakespeare's *Hamlet*, when

## BALLET WEAR

The classic male attire of doublet and hose became fairly standard ballet wear in the nineteenth century. The princely heroes of *Giselle* or *Swan Lake* are wearing almost exactly what Elizabethan courtiers wore, with the exception of the exaggerated padding, and for the same reason—it gives an elegant line, shows off a fine leg, and allows for athleticism and freedom of movement. Some items available from ballet suppliers are very suitable for Elizabethan costuming.

## MAKE IT—TRUNK HOSE

Cut a piece of cloth twice your waist measurement and one-and-a-half times the depth of your crotch measurement. Sew into a cylinder, leaving the seam open a short way at the bottom end. Lay the material flat and, with this seam in the center, cut a slit in the opposite side of the same length. Keeping the material flat, sew up the edges of the slits and across the end of seam to produce a pair of shorts. Hem the top edge and insert elastic or a drawstring. Repeat with the leg edges. Draw up the strings to produce a baggy, pouchy look.

*Right:* Sir Robert Shirley was envoy to the Shah of Persia in the early 1600s and was a walking advertisement for the silk trade he sought to manage.

Prince Hamlet appears to Ophelia with his stockings wrinkled, his doublet undone, and without a hat, she is truly shocked. Accessories were carefully assembled to suit each outfit—each "persona" in the living theater of life. Remember, however, that as a courtier or a member of the nobility, it's impossible to be overdressed. Today's fancy dress was everyday wear to an Elizabethan, and wearing last week's fashion was unpardonable.

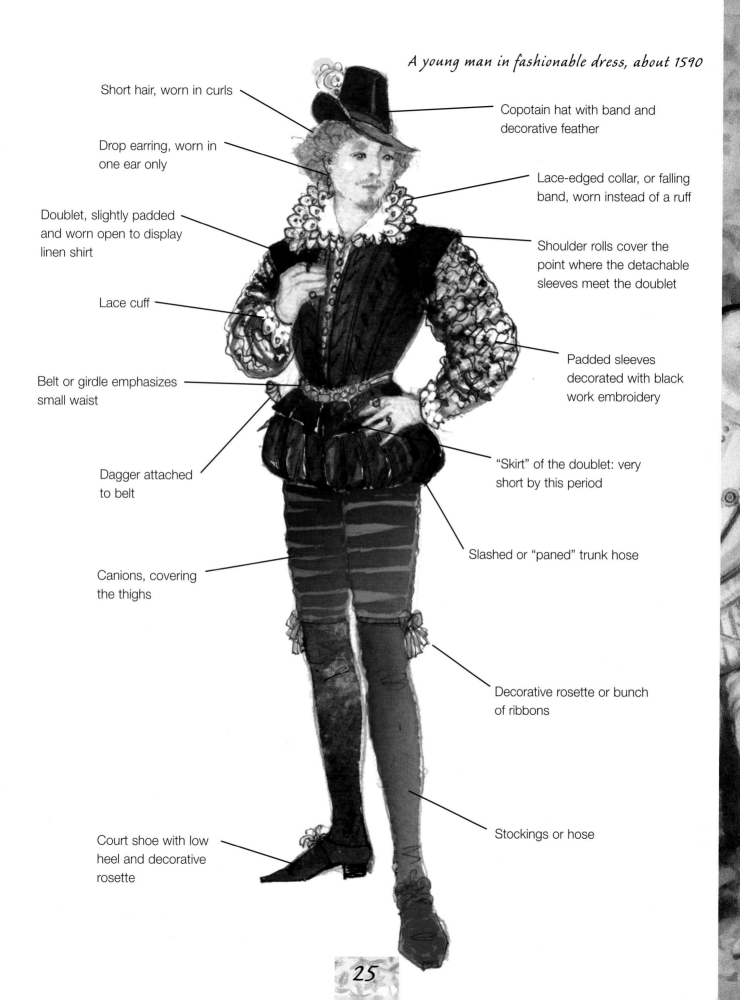

A young man in fashionable dress, about 1590

Short hair, worn in curls

Drop earring, worn in one ear only

Doublet, slightly padded and worn open to display linen shirt

Lace cuff

Belt or girdle emphasizes small waist

Dagger attached to belt

Canions, covering the thighs

Court shoe with low heel and decorative rosette

Copotain hat with band and decorative feather

Lace-edged collar, or falling band, worn instead of a ruff

Shoulder rolls cover the point where the detachable sleeves meet the doublet

Padded sleeves decorated with black work embroidery

"Skirt" of the doublet: very short by this period

Slashed or "paned" trunk hose

Decorative rosette or bunch of ribbons

Stockings or hose

## STYLE TIP

"He will come to her in yellow stockings, and 'tis a color she abhors, and cross-gartered, a fashion she detests." Clearly, the middle-class Malvolio has gotten both the color and the style wrong, but directors of Shakespeare's *Twelfth Night* have often duplicated his mistake by misinterpreting "cross-gartering." It doesn't mean winding the leg from ankle to thigh in criss-crossed ribbons, but tying a ribbon under the knee, winding it around the back of the leg, and tying in a big bow above the knee. Be warned: this style limits movement considerably!

## CHAPTER 4
# The Middle Classes and Professions

"All manners of attire came first into the city and the country from the court, which, being once received by the common people . . . the Courtiers justly cast off, and take new fashions." English traveler and writer Fynes Moryson (1617) was right about this: it was virtually impossible for most of the population to keep up with fashion.

## DOWN THE SOCIAL SCALE

The minor aristocracy, away from court and living in their country houses, followed court styles with less flashy fabrics, higher necklines, and longer doublets and fewer of the impractical accessories such as extreme ruffs and farthingales. With household luxuries such as curtains, cushions, and wall hangings more widespread, people needed fewer layers of clothing to keep warm. Wool, in all its various qualities, replaced the silk-based satins and brocades of the court for everyday wear, although anyone likely to be summoned to court had an outfit ready (and hoped it would not be too old-fashioned). We should not be fooled either by portraits showing people in their finery—obviously dressed in

*Above:* This Tudor re-enactment society re-creates a family gathering in a typical wood-paneled hall. Note that hats and caps are worn indoors.

26

their best for the occasion—or by movies in which people go about their country houses in silks. However, people always dressed to the best of their financial means.

## THE MIDDLING FOLK

A little farther down the scale came the thrusting, confident, newly emergent middle classes. They were determined to show off their newfound wealth—especially the women. For the first time, fairly ordinary people had the money and the opportunity to buy interesting clothes. On the whole, however, their style was quite conservative. "Certes, of all estates our merchants do least alter in their attire," remarked William Harrison, an English clergyman, in about 1577. Not only did fashions take time to reach the regions, but shops were few and far between.

Middle-class women either made their clothes themselves or ordered them from a local seamstress along with patterns, copied from court styles. Fabric was bought from a local haberdasher and came in different widths, depending on its type. Again, wool and linen were overwhelmingly the norm, although a silk dealer, or mercer, was on hand for the occasional luxury. Trimmings came into their own here, as they made up for the lack of fine material and could transform an old outfit. This was essential: decent fabric was too valuable to waste.

## FABRIC

Wool was so prevalent that it was often just referred to as "cloth," as in "a cloth gown." It came in all qualities and thicknesses. "Scarlet" meant wool of the finest quality, regardless of its color, although red was popular. Cotton was still virtually unknown in England: what is sometimes referred to as "cotton" is usually a fabric with the surface brushed into a soft pile. Fustian, which was made from wool, worsted, or flax, had this slight pile, which made it soft and suitable for hose. Velvet came in different weights.

Sometimes, when reproducing a costume, you get a better effect from a fabric that isn't exactly the right one. A decent quality plain cotton, especially the thicker, brushed variety, can give a more authentic look

*Above:* Al Pacino (right) as Shylock in a movie version of Shakespeare's *The Merchant of Venice* wears the fine wool clothing that suits his status as a wealthy businessman. The designer has also correctly given him the red cap that Venetian Jews of the period had to wear.

*Below:* In this production of *The Merry Wives of Windsor* the wives are wearing typically restrained wool outfits with white linen caps.

than a cheap wool blend, which will not only hang badly but will rub into pills. But avoid fabrics in a bright, modern color or with a printed pattern: these techniques were not yet available. If you are using wool, this should also be a solid color: no checks, tweeds, or modern prints. Also to be avoided are obvious modern inventions such as stretch velvets, velour, or jerseys—however comfortable they are—or anything knitted.

## COLOR AND DYEING

A true, deep black was very hard to fix in any fabric, and only the rich could afford it in any quantity. Respectable middle-class folk, however, had a single black gown or doublet for Sunday wear. Carefully saved, this outfit had probably outlasted other clothes and might be a little dated. Browns, grays, and pastels were also quite difficult to achieve and so were also the province of the better off. Most dyes were made from plants that were fairly common, such as madder (red) and woad (indigo), and these colors were accessible to all classes. Russet brown and green seem to have been popular choices for gowns among the middle classes, paired with creamy fine wool or linen for the kirtle.

## WHAT WOMEN WORE

Away from the court, a basic gown and kirtle were the standard wear. In her own home, a woman might omit the gown altogether and simply wear her wool kirtle around the house, slipping the gown on if visitors arrived. She would probably wear a partlet, a square of linen that

## A merchant couple, about 1580

Feathered hat, modeled on the copotain

Linen cap covering the hair

Small, simple ruff edged with black work to mimic real lace

Fitted doublet-style bodice of fine wool

Skirt worn over a bum roll to give the bell-shaped outline

Linen apron, decorated with white-work embroidery

Flat leather shoes

Flat wool cap in old-fashioned Tudor style

Short hair and beard neatly trimmed

Short cloak, with contrasting lining, worn over one shoulder

Doublet with contrasting, detachable sleeves

Jerkin, worn over the doublet

Venetians, tied at the knee with a garter

Worsted stockings

Flat leather shoes with rounded toes

## MAKE IT—A BUM ROLL

Use plain cotton drill or any non-stretch fabric. Take your waist measurement. Cut out two crescent-shaped pieces of cloth, using your waist as the inside measurement and adding 8 inches (20 cm) at the back and 5 inches (13 cm) at the sides. Taper the ends almost to a point. Sew around the edges, leaving an opening to turn the roll inside out, and clip the seams to ease the curve. Attach ribbons or strings at each end for tying. Turn inside out and stuff firmly until it's solid to the touch. Tie around the waist.

*Right:* Some scenes in *The Other Boleyn Girl* took place away from court. In the country, characters wore less ornate clothing, as Scarlett Johansson shows here with her simple dress, apron, and cap.

modestly filled in the neckline of a square-necked bodice and gathered into a small ruff. Few women wore full farthingales, but they achieved the same effect with a "bum roll": this was a stuffed, sausage-shaped roll tied around the waist under the skirt to hold it out from the waist. It was referred to as the poor woman's farthingale. However, middle-class women were notorious for giving their social aspirations free rein in the matter of dress, as one can see from many satirical writings. A good way of indicating comedy is to have a character overdressed or wearing one extreme fashion—a large ruff or farthingale, perhaps, or an elaborate hat.

## MIDDLE-CLASS MEN'S WEAR

The aim of a middle-class man was to look respectable, neat, and tidy. To this end, he would have worn a doublet of sensible cut and length— no slashing or peascod effect here— and clean white linen. His ruff would probably be quite discreet, fixed inside the standing collar of his doublet and just emerging above it. He probably wore knee-length Venetians rather than trunk hose and plain stockings under them, with stout leather shoes. Outdoors, he might wear a short cloak, like those worn indoors at court, and a neat hat.

*Above:* This soberly dressed man is William Cecil, Queen Elizabeth's chief advisor throughout her reign. This charming portrait shows him "off duty" and clad in the old-fashioned dress of a country gentleman.

## THE PROFESSIONS

In Protestant England, the clergy kept their rich and elaborately embroidered vestments for ceremonial occasions. For every day, a parish vicar would wear a plain, black cassock and over it a white sleeveless surplice. Doctors, lawyers, and other dignitaries retained the dark, wide-sleeved, fur-lined gown, developed from the medieval houppelande. These were always worn full length, as were ceremonial garments of any kind.

## WEDDINGS

There was no special bridal outfit, and white was not generally worn until the nineteenth century. Better-off women had a new gown made for their wedding, which would then be kept for special occasions; others simply wore their best. Brides often wore green because of its association with fertility. They also wore their hair loose, threaded with flowers, and carried a bridal wreath of roses and rosemary.

## FUNERAL BLACK

"Never did the English nation behold so much black worn as there was at her funeral," noted playwright Thomas Dekker at the funeral of Queen Elizabeth. Black had been the color of mourning since late medieval times, and the custom was studiously observed by the Elizabethans. The courtier-poet Sir Philip Sidney, who died of war wounds at the age of 31, was so well loved that for many months after his funeral it was considered indecent for any gentleman to appear at court or in the city of London "in any light or gaudy apparel."

*Right:* Elizabeth Taylor and Richard Burton, married in real life, made a handsome couple in the 1967 movie of *The Taming of the Shrew*. As we see here, however, the wedding dress was designed to show off Taylor's figure rather than to be authentic.

It was quite common for people to give items of clothing, particularly stockings and gloves, as presents and as tokens to celebrate weddings, christenings, and other special occasions. It's a good custom to revive if you're re-creating a period wedding.

## CLOTHES FOR MOURNING

Widows were expected to wear sober black for some time after the death of their husband. If they didn't marry again, this could be for the rest of their lives. They also removed their wedding bands. If you're costuming a family group, remember that there were far more elderly women than men in better-off Elizabethan society. Many contrived to look elegant in their black velvet "loose gowns" and caps. The celebrated Bess of Hardwick, who survived four husbands, was painted in her seventies as the Dowager Countess of Shrewsbury, looking calm and dignified.

## OUTDOOR WEAR

Men generally traveled on horseback and better-off women in a horse litter or a carriage—but since these did not have springs, they were hardly luxurious. Middle-class wives often rode sidesaddle behind their husbands. Men wore a long cloak over the doublet for riding, not the shorter cloak worn indoors, and perhaps some kind of leather or canvas jerkin for extra warmth. Movies of men riding in their shirts, other than at sports gatherings, are way off the mark. Men wore boots, knee or thigh length, but took them off on arrival: boots were never worn indoors. The low-heeled leather boots with straps and buckles, in fashion in the early twenty-first century, are a good choice for an outdoor outfit, but they should always be dull leather, not shiny. Modern riding boots are too streamlined. Women never wore boots, even for riding.

A woman would certainly wear a "safeguard," or overskirt, to protect her gown, and perhaps a mantle, a fur-trimmed sleeveless overcoat of wool or velvet. A wide, low-brimmed hat completed the outfit.

*Above:* Bess of Hardwick, one of the most powerful women of her generation, modeled her style of dress on that of the queen herself, whom she rather resembled.

# Countryfolk, Townsfolk, and Servants

*Above:* There are very few illustrations of country people, and the ones that do exist show them in rather fanciful costume, which is what the wealthy, or townspeople, believed they wore.

Generally, the dress of ordinary people was practical and sturdy, with very little decoration. It was also old-fashioned. They tried to maintain a neat and clean appearance, so mending and making do were high on the agenda, and clothing might be patched and frayed.

## COUNTRYFOLK

Many country dwellers were hardly touched by the changes from Tudor to Elizabethan. Their outfits hadn't changed much since medieval times. Men wore a thigh-length loose wool or linen smock and perhaps a canvas jerkin over it. Women wore a skirt and bodice, laced up the front, with a linen kirtle underneath and an apron tied around the waist. Both wore sturdy stockings of wool or worsted and flat leather shoes (or short, loose boots for men). In wet weather, wooden pattens or clogs were

fitted over the shoes to raise them out of the mud. "Start-ups" were a kind of high-fitting shoe plus leggings worn by outdoor workers.

For work in the fields, women tucked their long skirts up into their girdle. Aprons also could be looped up at the corners and tucked into the belt to form a bag for carrying produce. In hot weather, men sometimes rolled down their stockings and tied them under the knee with twine or, for rough work, wore another, shorter pair on top. However, going bare-legged anywhere except in the fields was not considered respectable. Only those in dire poverty did not wear stockings. Broad-brimmed straw hats (not boaters) were useful in the summer as protection from the sun in the open fields, and in winter men might wear a flat wool Tudor-style cap and women some kind of hood.

The color palette of ordinary people was limited to what they could dye themselves, so natural tones were the norm—brown, cream, russet, and green. All women could spin and sew, and many still made most of their family's clothing. They had wool from their own sheep and linen from flax grown in the garden, although neither would be of particularly good quality. Hemp, also grown domestically, produced an even rougher fabric, sometimes used for jerkins. When creating costume for a country character, choose fabrics with an obvious weave and texture.

*Above:* This re-enactment scene shows servants in the kitchen. Girls went into service at a fairly young age. These re-enactors are wearing plain, dyed wool clothes and white linen aprons.

*Above:* The costumes for the wives in the 2008 production of *The Merry Wives of Windsor* at Shakespeare's Globe Theater in London have some decorative touches in the fabric of the front-laced gowns.

Synthetics that look like linen, as long as they're not shiny, are fine for outer garments such as working smocks but not for shirts or underwear. Fabrics should be plain, solid colors: stripes and patterned material would not have been available to such folk. Smocking, in traditional designs, was worked on "best" tunics.

## TOWNSFOLK

Townspeople were better dressed than country dwellers. They might have bought their clothes rather than made them and could probably afford a decent hat. Women wore a plain wool gown, or skirt and bodice laced up the front over a plain kirtle and a partlet drawn up to resemble a ruff. Real ruffs and farthingales would be completely out of place in this environment. Most women, however, wore a white linen apron similar to that of their country counterparts. A popular hat for this class was a kind of derby, with a narrow brim.

Instead of a short doublet, the average townsman wore a plain fitted tunic or jerkin, which buttoned down the front. With this went either knee-length breeches (not padded or paned) or even just thick, plain stockings, depending on his job and status. As set out in the sumptuary laws, this also dictated whether he wore a hat or a wool cap.

## TRADESMEN AND APPRENTICES

Tradesmen, tailors, shopkeepers, and others who had a position to keep up wore the same clothing as townspeople but of better quality. Huntsmen, falconers, and anyone who interacted with the country aristocracy would also be better dressed than their neighbors. They were often given items of clothing by their employers so that they would look respectable in their company.

The village blacksmith and other manual workers wore distinctive aprons over their clothes: leather for the blacksmith,

*Left:* Huntsmen, who interacted with the aristocracy, often wore good-quality clothing provided by their employers.

*Below:* This young man, re-creating the character of an apprentice stonemason, is wearing the regulation wool cap required by statute.

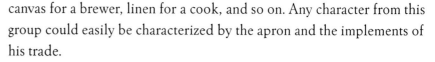
canvas for a brewer, linen for a cook, and so on. Any character from this group could easily be characterized by the apron and the implements of his trade.

Apprentices were given board and lodging with their master, who also supplied basic clothing. They would therefore wear ordinary clothes, as detailed above, probably mended and a little faded. A wool cap, as featured in the sumptuary laws, was essential.

## SERVANTS

In a big house, servants' clothing was part of their salary: they were given one new suit of clothes each year. This might be an ordinary gown or doublet and breeches or a complete set of clothing in the master's family colors. This was known as livery, and in most cases the family coat of arms was sewn onto their doublet.

*Below:* Much of Shakespeare's *Henry IV, Part 1*, takes place in a tavern. Here Prince Hal and Poins have dressed up as waiters in order to tease Falstaff. All they had to do was put on aprons and roll up their sleeves.

*Above:* These young re-enactors are playing with the simple wooden toys available to Elizabethan children, such as spinning tops.

Personal servants, such as ladies' maids and valets, often wore outfits handed down from their masters. Thus the outfits were slightly out of fashion but far better quality than the servants' own finances would allow. However, not all servants were poor: sometimes they were the younger children of minor aristocrats gaining experience of running a great house. Working-class servants—"tapsters" or "drawers" in inns, for example— wore the basic hose and jerkin or skirt and bodice in wool or linen, with white aprons. For authenticity, ale stains can be replicated with cold tea.

## CHILDREN AT WORK

Working-class or country children were at work from the time they could walk. A boy could scare birds from the crops, and little girls collected eggs, minded the next baby, or wound wool from their mother's spinning. There wasn't much time for play in these families, although illustrations show that they had basic toys such as hoops, dolls, and wooden animals.

Even quite young boys were collected by the press gangs who rounded up unwary men and conscripted them into the navy. They became cabin boys and learned to sail by being sent up the rigging. Others joined the army as drummer boys, although they often worked as general servants. They were regarded rather as mascots and were treated reasonably well when the men had time to look after them. Many, however, must have met the same sad end as the one in Kenneth Branagh's *Henry V,* murdered by the enemy. Any re-enactment should include at least one of these boys.

## COUNTRY PASTIMES

Any kind of country fair or gathering would attract crowds of local people and entertainers of all kinds. Morris dancers performed with sticks, streamers, and handkerchiefs; minstrels sang; and strolling players performed their dramas. Ballad mongers sold printed sheets of songs set to old tunes, which usually told of some recent scandal, a murder, or the hanging of a highwayman. Since their audience was mostly illiterate, they sang them to the crowd first.

The main attraction was the peddler, who brought cheap jewelry, ribbons, and trimmings, all eagerly snapped up by village girls. The word tawdry, meaning "cheap and gaudy," comes from "St. Audrey's Fair," a famous source of such stuff. All these characters are good for crowd scenes. They would be wearing standard clothing.

*Below:* This famous painting of a fair in Bermondsey, south London, around 1570 shows rich and poor mingling together. Their costumes clearly show which is which.

*Left:* Traveling peddlers wore stout, plain costume to combat all weathers. A leather or canvas jerkin kept the rain out, and a wide-brimmed hat provided shelter and shade.

## NAME THAT CLOTH

Cloth and particular colors were often popularly known by their place of origin. Damask, originally made in Damascus and discovered by the West at the time of the Crusades, is one that has lasted. Cambric came from Cambrai in France, muslin from Mosul in Iraq. Less exotic fabrics, made in England, include worsted, from Worstead in Norfolk. As with scarlet, the name of a cloth and its predominant color often got confused. Thus, Kendal green was a cloth worn by foresters in northern England—and, of course, by Robin Hood and his men—while Lincoln green was quite a different shade, produced in eastern England.

## THE FIELD OF THE CLOTH OF GOLD

This was a spectacular international "summit meeting," held in 1520 between Henry VIII of England and Francis I of France. Accompanied by thousands of knights and soldiers in ceremonial dress, they met on a plain outside Calais transformed for the occasion into a temporary town with huge golden tents and a palace with glass windows. There was jousting and fireworks, drinking and feasting, and a conspicuous display of finery on all sides. In a sermon that year, Bishop Fisher reflected on how the event got its name, describing how everyone was dressed "in rich clothes, in silks, velvets, cloths of gold, and such other precious raiments [garments]," accompanied by beautiful women "in sumptuous and gorgeous apparel." Not for the last time, fashion and politics went hand in hand.

# CHAPTER 6
# *Soldiers and Sailors*

Britain was a great seafaring nation. Marine adventurers such as Sir Francis Drake, Martin Frobisher, and Sir Walter Raleigh were much celebrated national heroes. However, anyone planning either plays or battle re-creation needs to consider the two sides of military life: the grand ceremonial occasions where everyone appears in finery, such as the

*Above:* Military commanders often had themselves painted in a combination of armor and fashionable court dress. Because of this, it's difficult to say exactly what soldiers and sailors wore in the field.

42

Field of the Cloth of Gold in Henry VIII's time, and the realities of war, which are usually much grimmer.

## TOURNAMENTS

The revival of the medieval tournament was an excuse for the nobility to dress up as knights—in armor already long out of date—and perform feats of arms. There was entertainment and feasting as well as jousting, in which two fully armed knights tried to unseat each other with long lances. Full metal armor, as worn by medieval knights, had become so heavy and cumbersome that it was hardly ever worn except on ceremonial occasions. Then it followed the style of civilian fashion, with breastplates shaped like peascod doublets and elaborate helmets. Soldiers in the field at most wore individual pieces of armor on arms, knees, and shoulders. The finest armor was imported from Italy and was highly ornate. Armor is notoriously difficult to replicate authentically, but cardboard sprayed with metallic paint gives a reasonable version of plate armor, while chain mail can be knitted from yarn and sprayed with the same.

## SOLDIERS

There was as yet no standing army in England. Men were recruited locally when war loomed, and they wore a rough approximation of a uniform in something like a buff jerkin, baggy knee-length breeches, and boots.

*Below:* These re-enactors are wearing bits and pieces of armor, just like real Elizabethan soldiers. Note the differences between the musket-man, the archer, and the man with the long lance, or pike.

*Above:* As we can see from the costumes, Falstaff was happy to take his recruits from all walks of life. Those with a little money, however, sometimes managed to buy their freedom.

Many, however, couldn't even manage this and went to war in little more than their ordinary clothes. The lucky ones had a cloak to wrap themselves up in at night. Shakespeare's *Henry IV* shows Falstaff callously recruiting country men and boys into the local militia at the threat of war, and his *Henry V* paints a vivid picture of army life in camp and on the field. Both are excellent sources for military characters.

## SAILORS

Although there was no specific naval uniform, the Admiralty did issue some clothing, perhaps creating a degree of uniformity. Sailors wore a canvas or leather jerkin over a shirt and waistcoat, slops (knee-length breeches), and flat shoes. Their clothes and hands would be stained with tar from the ropes. Strange naval headgear included the Monmouth cap, a knitted coif with hanging earflaps worn under a felted Tudor flat bonnet, and a distinctive plant-pot hat.

Canvas was good for clothing since it was water resistant and easily available. Indeed, in 1536 the French pilot of an English ship in Newfoundland was arrested for cutting up new sail canvas to make a jerkin and a pair of slops. Then as now, sailors would pick up odd items on their travels, so bits of jewelry, ornate buckles, fancy buttons, a feather

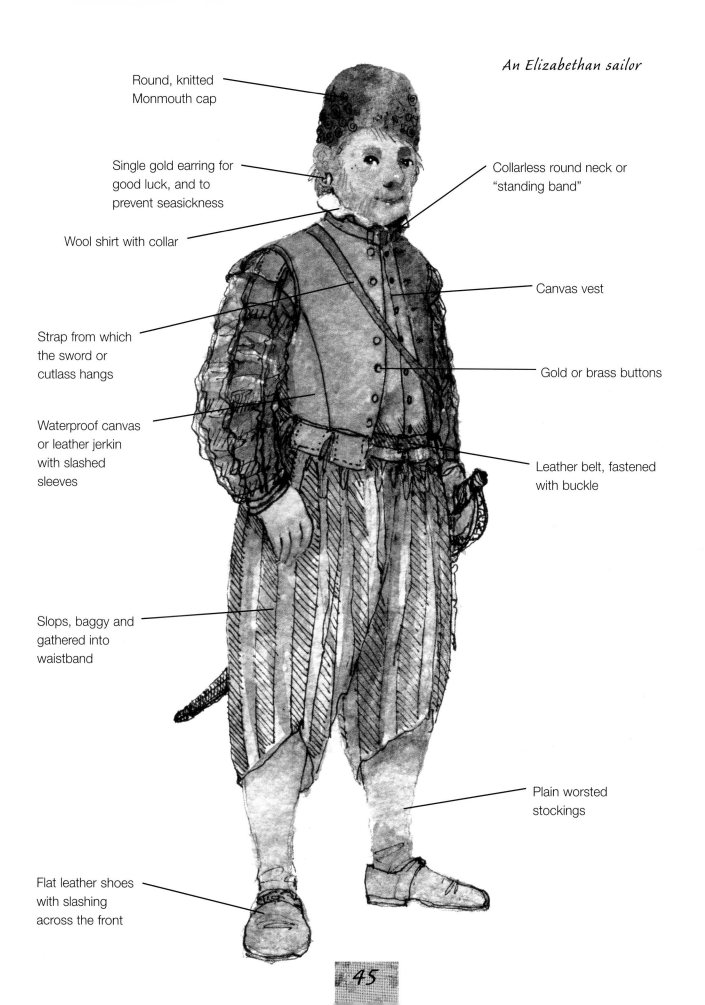

*An Elizabethan sailor*

Round, knitted Monmouth cap

Single gold earring for good luck, and to prevent seasickness

Wool shirt with collar

Strap from which the sword or cutlass hangs

Waterproof canvas or leather jerkin with slashed sleeves

Slops, baggy and gathered into waistband

Flat leather shoes with slashing across the front

Collarless round neck or "standing band"

Canvas vest

Gold or brass buttons

Leather belt, fastened with buckle

Plain worsted stockings

45

in the hat, and unusual scarves would not be out of place on a sailor character. A gold earring is also essential—thought to ward off seasickness. Thick cotton, or drill, can substitute for canvas and is more flexible, especially for breeches.

There was no age limit for soldiers and sailors. Even small boys were recruited into the navy as cabin boys and the army to guard provisions or tend horses. They wore cut-down versions of men's clothes.

## PIRATES

Pirates were usually sailors who found themselves unemployed in peacetime. They were a constant threat to shipping off the Spanish Main— the coast of the Caribbean and South America. Pirates dressed flamboyantly, flouting the sumptuary laws that bound citizens at home, most of their fine clothes having been stolen from the ships they boarded. A pirate captain might wear a fine linen shirt, a velvet doublet, and a silk waistcoat in crimson, violet, purple, or deep blue, with a silk sash, or baldric, slung across the chest. Crew members satisfied themselves with "motley" clothing—bright mismatched colors—and a bandanna around the head.

The image of pirates in thigh-high bucket boots and tricorn hats was one for the eighteenth century, but the extravagant style was established early. Women pirates, such as the famous Grace O'Malley, dressed as men since women were not allowed on board ship on pain of death.

*Left:* In keeping with their adventurous lives, sailors could be vain, although not all dressed as well as this French navigator.

## AFTERMATH OF WAR

England was renowned for the skill and bravery of its soldiers and sailors. However, terrible injuries and poor battlefield surgery meant that many ended their days as disabled beggars, showing off their stumps in the street. No production is complete without one of these sad reminders.

## THE WATCH

The Watch were a kind of local militia—patrols of armed citizens who went around the streets under the command of a constable. Although they did not wear any particular uniform, they were easily recognizable by what they carried: stout sticks, a spiked pole, a bell, and a lantern. The Watch in *Much Ado About Nothing*, led by Constable Dogberry, are the comedy stars of the show.

*Below:* There was no specific uniform for the Watch, but in this production of *Much Ado About Nothing*, Constable Dogberry has dressed his team in similar outfits. As team leader, however, he's given himself the best hat.

## THE POOR PRINCESS

Queen Elizabeth's love of fine clothing was perhaps a result of a deprived childhood. The daughter of Henry VIII and his second wife, Anne Boleyn, she grew up in the care of Lady Margaret Bryan at Hatfield House in the country. After her mother's execution, Princess Elizabeth was stripped of her title and neglected by her father. When the princess outgrew her baby clothes, Lady Bryan had to write to the king's minister, almost begging him for money to buy new, appropriate clothing: "for she hath neither gown, not kirtle nor sleeves, nor railes [nightgowns], nor body stitchets [corsets], nor handkerchiefs, nor mufflers nor biggins [caps]." No wonder Elizabeth made up for all this in adult life!

# CHAPTER 7
# *Children*

This was the first period in history in which children were considered important. Even though they were often treated as small adults, it's clear from records that they were much loved and treasured all the more because so many of them died in infancy. For this reason, families tended to have lots of children.

## BABIES AND TODDLERS

Babies were kept wrapped up in swaddling clothes for their first year, although this is not necessarily recommended for re-enactments! They

*Above:* This delightful christening portrait shows mother and baby dressed in their best clothes. Note the coral teething aid held by the child.

wore a linen cap or coif and might be clutching a teething ring, or stick, made of coral. This was also a symbol of good luck.

Boys and girls in better-off families were dressed alike until the age of four or five. They wore an ankle-length kirtle and gown, complete with hanging sleeves and streamers, by which they could be held while learning to walk. Some even had tiny replica hats, complete with feathers and jewels. Toddlers in poorer families, of course, made do with a simple smock and a rough tunic.

## TINY ADULTS

In general, children were dressed as miniature grown-ups. At about age five, boys were "breeched," that is, put into proper male clothing with breeches and a doublet. They even wore little daggers slung from the belt. Girls wore child-sized aprons over their increasingly fine gowns as they learned housewifery. Portraits show very young children wearing highly elaborate costumes, including ruffs, rigid bodices, and jewelry. These stiff garments must have been very restricting, although we are told that children did in fact run around, ride ponies, and get into trouble just as they do now. They always wore caps or coifs outdoors, with a proper hat on top when formally dressed.

*Below:* This portrait shows the family of Lord Cobham in 1567. The little girls are wearing miniature dresses, correct in every detail, and the boy on their left has a fine doublet. The two toddlers on the left, however, could be boys or girls. Unusually, they are all bare-headed.

*Right:* This young girl is clearly an aristocrat. Portraits like this were often painted to send to prospective bridegrooms. Note the highly elaborate sleeves, which are very unusual.

## YOUNG LADIES

Young girls were allowed to have their hair loose until their teenage years or until they married. After that, a woman was hardly ever seen with her hair down. In fact, it was unusual to see a woman with her head uncovered: coifs, caps, and hoods were almost always worn, even indoors.

## MAKING COSTUMES FOR CHILDREN

Here are a few tips about costuming young children. First, not many of them will want to be fastened into heavy, restricting clothes, so leave out the padding and boning. Keep it simple, even if it's not authentic. Use elastic or Velcro wherever possible instead of authentic but fussy ties. Use a sturdy fabric that's easily washable, but avoid the heaviness of furnishing fabrics, even though these look right. Go for dark, neutral colors that won't show dirt; fortunately, these are authentic. Allow for growth with generous hems and tucks that can be let out.

*A boy of about five years old and his sister*

Open tear-drop-shaped ruff in fine linen

Cap, covering the hair

Closed ruff in fine linen

Belt or girdle

Buttons close the bodice up to the neck

Her first "grown-up" gown: the bodice is stiffened with boning

Long, button-through gown, indicating that he's not quite old enough for doublet and breeches

Flat leather shoes

White linen apron to keep the gown clean

## THE FIRST SHOPPING MALL

In 1567, Sir Thomas Gresham opened the Royal Exchange in London. Originally planned as a center for commerce and trading, it was partly financed by renting out small shopping booths on the upper floors. In no time, the Exchange had become not only the place for one-stop shopping but also a fashionable meeting place. Ready-made clothing, accessories, and luxury goods of all kinds were widely available for the first time. In 1571, the queen attended the official opening and gave the Exchange its royal title.

# CHAPTER 8

# *Accessories*

In image-conscious Elizabethan society, accessories were of major importance, and they are an excellent way of differentiating characters in re-enactments today. Style leaders prided themselves on sourcing goods from as many different places as possible, which, as an anonymous sixteenth-century writer noted, included a French doublet, German hose, a Spanish hat and sword, an Italian ruff, and shoes made in Flanders.

*Above:* Archery was popular with women, as shown in this production of Shakespeare's *Love's Labour's Lost*. Jaunty little "pipkin" hats were perfect for outdoor sports.

52

However, this was seen as encouraging a taste for foreign luxuries instead of supporting local industries, and sumptuary laws were passed in an attempt to regulate people's extravagance. As with fabrics, always make sure your characters are only wearing something they are entitled to!

## HATS

There were various coverings for the hair. A coif, or "biggin," was a plain linen cap that fit close to the head. A caul was a simple circle of linen or net gathered onto a band. It sat toward the back of the head, with the hair pulled back into it. Both are quite easy to make. Either of them might be worn alone—casually, at home—but mostly they were worn with a hat or hood pinned on top. Tudor hoods and flat caps were now out of fashion although still worn in the provinces. Hats, usually small and jaunty, were very much the style.

Most typical is the taffeta pipkin, a little round hat that sat neatly on the head, slightly forward. Immensely popular, it was worn at court, in town, or in the provinces, in various fabrics and trimmed to match a gown.

For men, hats with brims and crowns replaced the soft cap style of the Tudors. The most popular was the copotain, a stiff, tall-crowned hat with a small upturned brim, trimmed with buttons, pins, or perhaps a feather and worn slightly askew on the head.

## STOCKINGS

Brightly colored, hand-knitted, and embroidered, or "clocked" at the ankle, stockings were very valuable items. They were high on the list of gifts given to Queen Elizabeth for New Year's. The best were made of

*"*More light than the lightest French, and more sumptuous than the proudest Persians . . . they have worn out all the fashions of France and all the nations of Europe . . . yea, the tailors and shopkeepers daily invent fantastical fashions for hats, and like new fashions and names for stuffs. *"*

Fynes Moryson, *An Itinerary* (1617)

*Right:* Bette Davis was one of the first actresses to portray Queen Elizabeth, in the 1939 movie *Elizabeth and Essex*. Note the "shaved" hairline, although it's almost certain that this was achieved with a "bald" wig.

silk, but worsted ones were worn for every day and sometimes also under the silk pair for extra warmth. The variety of colored tights available today means this is the easiest part of a costume to source, for both sexes.

## HAIR AND MAKEUP

As coifs and hoods were gradually abandoned, hairstyles became more important. Golden hair was much admired and was often achieved by dyeing. Hair was worn braided behind the head and teased out over a

*Left:* The dashing Earl of Essex was a real dandy and is seen here with the latest style of forked beard combed neatly over his ruff.

## STYLE TIP

Whatever you do, don't wear your best silk gloves or use your handkerchief! Both of these were considered to be luxury items and were meant only to be held in the hand or tucked into the belt. Handkerchiefs of silk or linen were embroidered and lace-edged. Gloves were gauntlet style, highly embroidered on the back and on the wrist part, the edges trimmed with lace or gold filigree. Gloves and handkerchiefs, along with stockings and even shoes, were perfumed, often with rose or orange water.

high forehead, itself usually emphasized by shaving or plucking the hairline. As the century wore to a close, court hairstyles became more and more artificial. Tall wigs or one's own hair padded with horsehair stuffing were studded with brooches on wire pins called hair bodkins. However, most ordinary women kept their hair long, braided around the ears or pulled up into a bun held in a decorative caul.

Men's hair was usually worn short, with beards and mustaches neatly trimmed. The appearance was generally neat and tidy, if rather formal.

Elizabethan makeup involved highly dangerous concoctions of mercury, lead, and other toxic substances. Fortunately, commercially available makeup avoids this risk to health today. The goal is to be pale, with rouged cheeks, kohl-rimmed eyes, and red lips.

*Right:* Pearls were the queen's favorite adornment because they were a symbol of virginity. Here she wears them as "teardrops" sewn to her clothing and in her hair, as well as around her neck in ropes.

*Right:* The Barbor Jewel, with a cameo of the queen in the center, is a typical pendant brooch.

# JEWELRY

Pile on the jewelry: the Elizabethans wore gold chains, necklaces, brooches, pins, rings, and earrings, not to mention the pearls, glass beads, and gemstones sewn onto the clothing itself.

Brooches and pins were worn on the gown or doublet, on hatbands, and in the hair. They combined gold, enamel, and precious stones, set in the shape of galleons, animals, and insects. The salamander was particularly popular since it suggested continuity. Galleons were another popular choice, recalling victories at sea.

Jeweled animal brooches (but no poodles or pussycats!) can often be found in costume jewelry shops, and cheap glass or plastic beads are good for sewing onto fabric. But sew them firmly. Queen Elizabeth was forever losing hers, as her wardrobe mistress recorded. The queen's loss was to be our gain, however, since we now have excellent documentary evidence of what went missing.

Older men still wore the heavy gold chains of the Tudors, often several at once in different lengths. Remember that chains were often given as gifts or signs of approval to inferiors. Women, however, followed the queen's taste and wore long ropes of pearls and single pearls on bodkins in the hair.

Pendants hung from chains around the neck or from chokers. The simplest was a single large jewel or pearl, surrounded with smaller gems in either a square or a round setting. The very popular double pendants

## STYLE TIP

Wearing your wealth so conspicuously had its drawbacks. Jewels sewn onto clothing often came unstitched. The royal accounts are full of notes about precious stones lost from Queen Elizabeth's gowns. These included one of several large gold-enameled blue pendants from a purple velvet gown; a pearl and a gold tassel from "a French gown of black satin" worn at Greenwich; one of twelve small rubies set in gold on a hat band; a small golden acorn and one oak leaf, lost at Westminster; and two buttons shaped like golden tortoises with pearl eyes. The moral is, use a strong thread, and don't wear anything you'd mind losing.

featured the family initials, worked in gold or tiny gems, with some other shape—an animal or galleon, perhaps—linked beneath. Cameos and miniature portraits of relatives were also popular as pendants or brooches. It's fun to customize your own pendant from modeling clay and plastic "gems."

Earrings were quite small and discreet: a single pearl or precious-gem drop, perhaps. Hoops or long, dangling earrings are out—not least because they would get tangled up in the ruff. Clip-ons are, of course, anachronistic but handy. Rings were worn on the first finger and sometimes on the thumb—sometimes on every finger. However, it's rare to see a single wedding band on the fourth finger.

Obviously, such jewelry is decoration for the wealthy alone. Rich merchants and their wives had the same styles made up in garnets or moonstones and nonprecious metals such as pewter, but the lower classes hardly had so much as a wedding ring. A cheap necklace of wooden beads or a brightly colored ribbon around the neck would be all a country girl could afford.

*Right:* Gloves like this one, of kidskin and lace, were never put to any practical use. For extra ornamentation, rings were often worn over the glove.

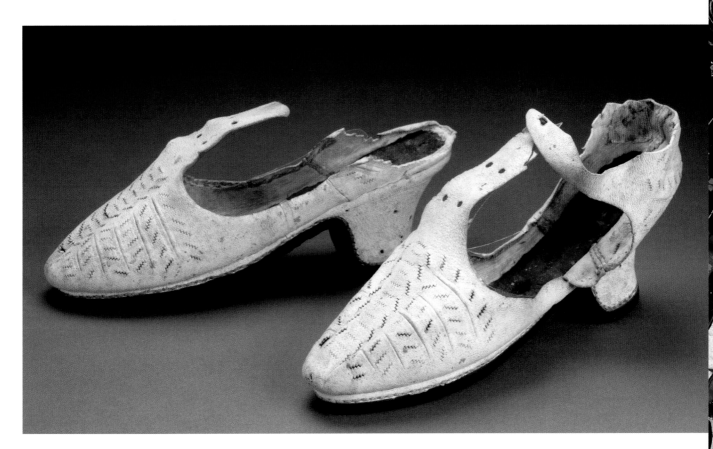

*Above:* This pair of ladies' shoes in white leather is a remarkable survival. Note the small heel.

## SHOES

Tudor shoes were completely flat and, in Henry's day, fashionably wide—a statute limited them to about six inches (15 centimeters)—with patterns punched out in the fronts. These remained in fashion, although becoming narrower, until low heels were introduced toward the 1590s. Outdoor shoes were made of leather, indoor ones of velvet, dyed to match an outfit. Like clothing, leather shoes were slashed to reveal the colored stockings beneath, while fabric ones were embroidered. They look rather like espadrilles, which might make a good substitute if suitably embroidered. Pantofles were high cork-soled shoes, notoriously hard to walk in. Standing on one's pantofles indicated pride—like being on your high horse.

## BITS AND PIECES

Since clothes still didn't have pockets, accessories were attached to the belt or girdle. These might include small notebooks, prayer books, keys, fans, daggers, perfume bottles, and pomanders—perforated containers filled with sweet-smelling herbs.

## SHOES

Even footwear came under the stern disapproval of Philip Stubbes in his *Anatomy of Abuses*. The popular cork-soled shoes and pantofles that raised people several inches off the ground were a particular target. Although they were mostly made of leather, he was shocked to find some made of more exotic velvet, in colors such as black, white, red, or green, and "carved, cut and stitched all over with silk, and laid on with gold, silver and such like." He also noted, with some satisfaction, that walking in them was hard work.

# Glossary

**bride laces** Laces of gold silk used to tie nosegays in the hats of wedding guests.

**brocade** Any rich, stiff silk fabric with a pattern woven into it.

**buckram** A stiff cotton or linen fabric used for lining garments.

**canions** Close-fitting, knee-length breeches.

**canvas** A coarse cloth made of hemp or linen.

**cassock** A long garment worn by clergymen.

**clocking** Embroidery, usually in a circular pattern, on the ankle of a stocking.

**cloth of gold** A fabric woven with real gold thread.

**coat of arms** The badge of a noble family.

**codpiece** A flap of cloth covering the gap at the top of men's hose.

**coif** A close-fitting cap of white linen tied under the chin, worn by both sexes.

**copotain** A tall-crowned, narrow-brimmed hat, worn by both men and women.

**cotehardie** A long, body-hugging garment for women.

**damask** A reversible, patterned fabric made of linen, silk, or wool.

**doublet** A short, quilted, or padded jerkin with a front opening, worn by men from the fourteenth century on.

**drill** Strong, hard-wearing cotton.

**falconer** A man who trains and flies birds of prey.

**flax** A blue-flowered plant whose fibrous stems are made into cloth.

**flocks** Lumps of fabric waste.

**fustian** Coarse cloth of brushed cotton weft and linen warp.

**gable headdress** An English hood shaped like the pointed gable of a house.

**galleon** A large sailing ship.

**gauntlet** A glove with a long cuff.

**holland** Linen cloth.

**houppelande** A voluminous costume, worn by both men and women, with wide, hanging sleeves and either a high stand-up collar or a V neck.

**jerkin** A sleeveless fitted jacket.

**lace** A small cord or tie, or a web-like fabric.

**lawn** A fine, sheer linen or cotton fabric of plain weave.

**mail** (or **chain mail**) Armor made of interlocking rows of metal rings.

**mantle** A loose sleeveless cloak.

**miniver** The grayish white fur of a squirrel.

**pantofle** A cork-soled backless shoe.

**partlet** A blouse covering the neck and shoulders with a standing collar and full long sleeves.

**pattens** Raised wooden soles attached to shoes to keep them out of the mud.

**peascod** A doublet that was padded to a point at the waist and swelled over the girdle.

**russet** A reddish brown color; also, a coarse wool cloth worn by country people.

**selvage** The edge on either side of a woven or flat-knitted fabric to prevent raveling.

**surplice** A loose white outer church vestment, usually knee length with large open sleeves.

**swaddling** Wrapping a young child in strips of linen.

**taffeta** A thin, stiff fabric.

**train** The extended hem of a dress that trails on the ground.

**velvet** A soft, thick-piled fabric of silk or cotton.

**white work** White embroidery on white fabric.

**worsted** A wool fabric with a smooth surface and no nap.

# Further Information

## BOOKS

Arnold, Janet. *A Handbook of Costume.* Macmillan, 1973.

Arnold, Janet. *Patterns of Fashion: The Cut and Construction of Clothes for Men and Women, c.1560–1620.* Drama Publishers, 1985.

Arnold, Janet. *Queen Elizabeth's Wardrobe Unlock'd.* Quite Specific Media Group, 2001.

Covet, Liz, and Rosemary Ingham. *The Costume Designer's Handbook.* Heinemann Drama, 1992.

Dearling, Shirley. *Elegantly Frugal Costumes: The Poor Man's Do-It-Yourself Costume Maker's Guide.* Meriwether, 1992.

Elgin, Kathy. *Elizabethan England: A History of Costume and Fashion.* Facts On File, 2005.

Haley, Gail E. *Costumes for Plays and Playing.* Parkway, 2002.

Hunnisett, Jean. *Period Costume for Stage & Screen: Patterns for Women's Dress 1500–1800.* Players Press, 1991.

Kidd, Mary. *Stage Costume, Step by Step.* Betterway Books, 2002.

Mikhaila, Ninya. *The Tudor Tailor: Reconstructing Sixteenth-Century Dress.* Costume & Fashion Press, 2006.

Norris, Herbert. *Tudor Costume and Fashion.* Dover, 1997.

Pecktal, Lynn. *Costume Design: Techniques of Modern Masters.* Backstage Books, 1999.

Tierney, Tom. *Elizabethan Costumes Paper Dolls.* Dover, 1996.

Tierney, Tom. *Tudor and Elizabethan Fashions.* Dover, 2000.

Winter, Janet, and Carolyn Savoy. *Elizabethan Costuming for the Years 1550–1580.* Other Times Publications, 1987.

## WEB SITES

Many of these Web sites have links to other, related sites.

**www.blackworkarchives.com**
Has information on black work embroidery and free printable patterns.

**www.costumes.org**
The Costumers Manifesto, a general Web site on the history of costume. The Elizabethan page within the site is at: www.costume.org/history/100pages/ costhistpage.html.

**www.elizabethancostume.net**
Probably the best site dedicated to costume of the period, with information on costume, research sources, tips on re-creating costume, use of fabric, and some easy patterns.

**www.elizabethangeek.com**
Database of portraits and costume images with notes and commentary.

**www.fordham.edu/halsall/medfilms.html**
A list of films with historical themes up to the sixteenth century.

**www.fordham.edu/halsall/mod/1577harrison-england.html**
Tudor history sourcebook, including Harrison's *Description of England.*

**www.nationalarchives.gov.uk**
Links to the wardrobe accounts of Henry VIII and Queen Elizabeth I.

**www.sempstress.org**
Has patterns and instructions.

**www.simplicity.com**
Simplicity Patterns has a historical collection.

**www.vertetsable.com**
The Renaissance Tailor offers patterns and instructions drawn from sixteenth- and seventeenth-century pattern books.

# Source List

A selection of plays, operas, movies, and TV series with Tudor and Elizabethan themes.

## TUDOR

### PLAYS

*Henry VIII*, by William Shakespeare

*A Man For All Seasons* (1960), by Robert Bolt (the story of Sir Thomas More)

### OPERA

*Anna Bolena* (1830), by Gaetano Donizetti

*Henry VIII* (1883), by Camille Saint-Saëns

### MOVIES

*Anne of the Thousand Days* (1969), dir. Charles Jarrott, with Richard Burton, Geneviève Bujold

*Lady Jane* (1986), dir. Trevor Nunn, with Helena Bonham Carter, Cary Elwes

*A Man For All Seasons* (1966), dir. Fred Zinnemann, with Paul Scofield, Wendy Hiller

*The Other Boleyn Girl* (2008), dir. Justin Chadwick, with Natalie Portman, Scarlett Johansson

*The Private Life of Henry VIII* (1933), dir. Alexander Korda, with Charles Laughton, Elsa Lanchester

### TV

*Henry VIII* (2003), dir. Pete Travis, with Ray Winstone, Helena Bonham Carter (TV series)

*A Man For All Seasons* (1988), dir. Charlton Heston, with Vanessa Redgrave, Charlton Heston

*The Six Wives of Henry VIII* (1973), dir. various, with Keith Michell, Dorothy Tutin (TV series)

*The Tudors* (2007), dir. various, with Jonathan Rhys Meyers, Natalie Dormer (TV series)

## ELIZABETHAN

### PLAYS

*Elizabeth the Queen* (1930), by Maxwell Anderson

*Maria Stuart* (1800), by Friedrich Schiller (about Queen Elizabeth and Mary, Queen of Scots)

*The Merry Wives of Windsor*, by William Shakespeare

*Romeo and Juliet*, by William Shakespeare (plus various ballet versions of the play)

*Rosencrantz and Guildenstern Are Dead* (1966), by Tom Stoppard

Shakespeare's plays, especially the comedies, are often staged in "traditional" Elizabethan style although they are not necessarily set in that period. This is especially true of the comedies, such as *The Taming of the Shrew* and *As You Like It*. Conversely, many Elizabethan works are given "modern dress" makeovers.

### OPERA

*Falstaff* (1893), by Guiseppe Verdi

*Gloriana* (1953), by Benjamin Britten

*Maria Stuarda* (1835), by Gaetano Donizetti (based on the Schiller play)

### MOVIES

*Les Amours de la Reine Élisabeth* (1912), dir. Henri Desfontaines, Louis Mercanton, with Sarah Bernhardt, Lou Tellegen

*Chimes at Midnight* (1966), dir. Orson Welles, with Orson Welles, John Gielgud (a version of Shakespeare's *Henry IV*)

*Il Dominatore dei Sette Mari* (*Seven Seas to Calais*, 1962), dir. Rudolph Mate, Primo Zeglio, with Rod Taylor, Irene Worth

*Drake of England* (1935), dir. Arthur B. Woods, with Matheson Lang, Athene Seyler

*Elizabeth* (1998), dir. Shekhar Kapur, with Cate Blanchett, Joseph Fiennes

*Elizabeth: The Golden Age* (2007), dir. Shekhar Kapur, with Cate Blanchett, Clive Owen

*Fire Over England* (1937), dir. William K. Howard, with Flora Robson, Laurence Olivier

*Mary of Scotland* (1936), dir. John Ford, with Katharine Hepburn, Fredric March

*Mary, Queen of Scots* (1971), dir. Charles Jarrott, with Vanessa Redgrave, Glenda Jackson

*The Merchant of Venice* (2004), dir. Michael Radford, with Al Pacino, Jeremy Irons

*Orlando* (1992), dir. Sally Potter, with Tilda Swinton, Quentin Crisp

*The Prince and the Pauper* (1962), dir. William Keighley, with Errol Flynn, Claude Rains

*The Private Lives of Elizabeth and Essex* (1939), dir. Michael Curtiz, with Bette Davis and Errol Flynn

*La Reine Margot* (1994), dir. Patrice Chéreau, with Isabelle Adjani, Daniel Auteuil

*Romeo and Juliet* (1968), dir. Franco Zeffirelli, with Olivia Hussey, Leonard Whiting

*The Sea Hawk* (1940), dir. Michael Curtiz, with Flora Robson, Errol Flynn

*Shakespeare in Love* (1998), dir. John Madden, with Joseph Fiennes, Gwyneth Paltrow

*The Sword and the Rose* (1953), dir. Ken Annakin, with Glynis Johns, James Robertson Justice

*The Taming of the Shrew* (1967), dir. Franco Zeffirelli, with Elizabeth Taylor, Richard Burton

*The Virgin Queen* (1923), dir. J. Stuart Blackton, with Lady Diana Manners

*The Virgin Queen* (1955), dir. Henry Koster, with Bette Davis, Richard Todd

*Young Bess* (1953), dir. George Sidney, with Jean Simmons, Charles Laughton

**TV**

*Blackadder II*, (1986), dir. Mandie Fletcher, with Rowan Atkinson, Miranda Richardson (a comedy series set in the Elizabethan period)

*Elizabeth* (2000), dir Steven Clarke, Mark Fielder (documentary drama presented by David Starkey)

*Elizabeth I* (2005), dir. Tom Hooper, with Helen Mirren, Jeremy Irons (mini-series)

*Elizabeth I: The Virgin Queen* (2005), dir. Tom Hooper, with Anne-Marie Duff, Ian Hart

*Elizabeth R* (1971), dir. Roderick Graham, Richard Martin, with Glenda Jackson (mini-series)

*Elizabeth Rex* (2003), dir. Barbara Willis Sweete, with Diane D'Aquila

*Gunpowder, Treason and Plot* (2004), dir. Gillies MacKinnon, with Robert Carlyle, Catherine McCormack (a mini-series about Mary, Queen of Scots and James I)

Many of the movies and TV series are available on DVD. Also available are various TV and movie versions of Shakespeare plays, some of which are set in the Elizabethan period.

# Index